WHAT HAPPENS AFTER PASCAL'S WAGER

LIVING FAITH AND RATIONAL BELIEF

THE AQUINAS LECTURE, 2009

WHAT HAPPENS AFTER PASCAL'S WAGER

LIVING FAITH AND RATIONAL BELIEF

DANIEL GARBER

MARQUETTE
UNIVERSITY
PRESS

© 2009 Marquette University Press
Milwaukee, Wisconsin 53201-3141
All rights reserved.
www.marquette.edu/mupress/

Under the auspices of the
Wisconsin-Alpha Chapter of Phi Sigma Tau

Library of Congress Cataloging-in-Publication Data
Garber, Daniel, 1949-
  What happens after Pascal's wager : living faith and rational
belief / Daniel Garber.
    p. cm.
"The Aquinas lecture, 2009."
Includes bibliographical references.
  ISBN-13: 978-0-87462-176-1 (clothbound : alk. paper)
  ISBN-10: 0-87462-176-3 (clothbound : alk. paper)
1. Pascal, Blaise, 1623-1662. Pensées. 2. Knowledge, Theory
of (Religion) 3. Faith and reason—Christianity. 4. Christian
life—Catholic authors. I. Title.
  B1901.P43G37 2009
  231'.042—dc22

                                          2008053919

Printed in the United States of America.

Association of American
University Presses

MARQUETTE UNIVERSITY PRESS
MILWAUKEE

The Association of Jesuit University Presses

The Wisconsin-Alpha Chapter of Phi Sigma Tau, the International Honor Society for Philosophy at Marquette University, each year invites a scholar to deliver a lecture in honor of St. Thomas Aquinas.

The 2009 Aquinas Lecture, *What Happens after Pascal's Wager: Living Faith and Rational Belief* was delivered on Sunday, February 23, 2009, by Daniel Garber, Chair and Professor of Philosophy at Princeton University.

Daniel Garber studied Philosophy at Harvard University, receiving his Ph.D. in 1975. He taught

at the University of Chicago from 1975-2002. From 1995-2002 he was Lawrence Kimpton Distinguished Service Professor in Philosophy, and a member of the Committee on Conceptual and Historical Studies of Science, and the Morris Fishbein Center for the Study of History of Science and Medicine. In 2002 he moved to Princeton University, where he has been Chair of the Department since 2005. Prof. Garber has held visiting appointments at the University of Minnesota, Johns Hopkins University, Princeton's Institute for Advanced Study, École Normale Supérieure (Lettres) (Lyon, France), and the University of Oxford (Faculty of Philosophy and Corpus Christi College), where he was Isaiah Berlin Visiting Professor. Among numerous honors and awards, Prof. Garber has received several NEH grants, an ACLS Fellowship, and the Faculty Award for Excellence in Graduate Teaching at the University of Chicago.

Prof. Garber has been a prolific scholar. He has authored two books, *Descartes' Metaphysical Physics* and *Descartes Embodied: Reading Cartesian Philosophy through Cartesian Science*. Both of those books have been translated into French. In addition, he co-edited (with Michael Ayers) the two volume *Cambridge History of Seventeenth-Century Philosophy*, and has edited or co-edited several other books, including a collection of translations of texts by Leibniz and, most recently, a collection of essays entitled *Kant and the Early Moderns*. He has two books forthcoming: a monograph entitled *Leibniz: Body, Substance, Monad* to be published by Oxford University Press and a collection of essays on the history of the mechanical philosophy in the seventeenth century to be published in the series *Boston Studies in the Philosophy of Science*. Prof. Garber has published more than eighty journal articles and book chapters covering many figures in the history of modern philosophy, including Descartes, Spinoza, Leibniz, Locke and Berkeley. In addition, he has published essays on the history of science, Aristotelianism in the seventeenth century, an several articles on the practice and value of historical scholarship in philosophy. His 1989 essay "Does History have a Future? Some Reflections on Bennett and Doing Philosophy Historically" influenced a generation of younger scholars. His more recent essays "Toward an Antiquarian History of Philosophy" and "What's Philosophical about the History of Philosophy?" provide rich additions to the literature on the value of history to philosophy.

Prof. Garber's service to the profession is especially notable. He is Co-editor (with Steven Nadler), of *Oxford Studies in Early-Modern Philosophy*, Associate Editor of the *New Synthese Historical Library* (Springer), a member of the Board of Editors of *Oxford Studies in the History of Philosophy*, and *Perspectives on Science*, a member of the Board of Advisors of *The Cambridge Dictionary of Philosophy* and the *Lexicon Philosophicum* (Lessico

Intellectuale Europeo e Storia delle Idee, Rome), and a Consulting Editor of *Studies in History and Philosophy of Science* and the *British Journal for the History of Philosophy.*

To Prof. Garber's distinguished list of publications, Phi Sigma Tau is pleased to add: *What Happens after Pascal's Wager: Living Faith and Rational Belief.*

WHAT HAPPENS AFTER PASCAL'S WAGER

LIVING FAITH AND RATIONAL BELIEF

DANIEL GARBER
Princeton University

The wager argument occupies a pivotal role in Pascal's *Pensées*.[1] And a dramatic moment it is. Pascal convinces the libertine that in this life, he is forced to wager on God's existence:

> ... Either God is or he is not. But to which side shall we incline? ... There is an infinite chaos that separates us. At the extremity of this infinite distance, a game is being played in which heads or tails will turn up. How will you wager? [S680/L418][2]

---

1 Vincent Carraud objected to this after an oral presentation. Certainly, on some readings of the apologetic project of the *Pensées*, the wager may not play a central role. But on other plausible readings it certainly does. In any case, the larger structure of Pascal's apologetic project isn't really central for my paper.

2 References to Pascal's *Pensées* are given in two current editions, based on two different manuscript sources. 'S' refers to the numbering in Blaise Pascal, *Pensées*, ed. Philippe Sellier (Paris: Livre de Poche, 2000); 'L' refers to the numbering in Pascal, *Oeuvres completes*, ed. Louis

He then convinces the libertine that the wise choice is to bet on God. If he believes that God exists, and he does indeed exist, then the libertine gains eternal happiness; if God doesn't exist, then the libertine loses nothing, even in this life. But if he fails to believe in God, then the libertine loses everything.

I don't want to offer yet another analysis of this famous argument, neither a defense nor an attack. Rather, I would like to look at what happens after the argument is over. Suppose the libertine (me, for example) accepts Pascal's reasoning, and I decide that I want to believe in God. What then? Pascal knows perfectly well that belief is not voluntary; unlike raising my arm, I can't will to believe and expect that genuine faith will follow. He suggests that I follow a regimen, go to mass, take holy water, act like a believer and belief will follow. In fact, when I reach this final state, Pascal claims, my belief will be *rational*: at the end of the process that results in my having faith, he claims, I will be able to see real reasons for believing that may have been hidden to me before.

Despite the apparent rationality of the belief that comes out of this process, I have a lingering suspicion that there is something fishy going on here. This, then, is my question: when I reach the

---

Lafuma (Paris: Éditions du Seuil, 1963). The translations are taken from Pascal, *Pensées*, ed. and trans. Roger Ariew (Indianapolis: Hackett, 2005). Ariew follows the Sellier text.

end state of the Pascal Regimen, and have faith in God grounded in reasons, am I really entitled to belief? I have what under normal circumstances would appear to be a rational belief. But should I really trust it?

BEGINNINGS: PASCAL'S CLAIMS

Let me begin by outlining the elements of Pascal's position that are relevant to my question.

One way of convincing someone to be a Christian would be to give that person reasons, arguments, some rational motivation for adopting the position under consideration. But, Pascal claims, reason and experience can never lead us to real belief. Pascal is deeply pessimistic about the ability of reason taken by itself to lead us to any real understanding of the way the world is:

> Ludicrous. reason, blowing with the wind in every direction! … Anyone who chose to follow reason alone would have proved himself a fool. [S78/ L44][3]

Experience isn't much help either, for Pascal. While there are dim indications of the Deity in nature, they are not clear enough to give us definite reason to believe in his existence:

---

3   The second sentence in this quotation appears in L but not S.

I look in all directions and see only darkness everywhere. Nature offers me nothing that is not a matter
of doubt and concern. If I saw nothing in it that
revealed a divinity, I would come to a negative conclusion; if I saw everywhere the signs of a creator, I
would settle down peacefully in faith. But, seeing too
much to deny and too little to reassure me, I am in a
pitiful state, in which I have wished a hundred times
that if a God maintains nature, it should proclaim
him unequivocally, and that if the signs it gives
are deceptive, it should suppress them altogether;
nature should say all or nothing, that I might see
which side I ought to take. [S682/L429]

And so Pascal would seem to reject naturalistic
proofs for the existence of God:

"Why, do you not yourself say that the sky and the
birds prove God?" No. "And does not your religion
say so?" No. For while this is true in a sense for some
souls to whom God gave this illumination, nevertheless it is false for most of them. [S38/L3]

In our fallen state, separated from God, I am incapable of reaching God through my natural faculties,
reason and experience:

Man is but a subject full of natural error that cannot
be eradicated without grace. [Nothing] shows him
the truth. Everything deceives him. ... These two
principles of truth, reason and the senses, besides
both lacking authenticity, mutually deceive one
another. [S78/L45]

This is the starting place of the wager argument,
a world in which it is not possible to determine

whether or not there is a God through my rational faculties alone:

> Let us then examine this point and say: either God is or he is not. But to which side shall we incline? Reason can determine nothing here. … Reason is no more offended by choosing one rather than the other. [S680/L418]

And so, Pascal proceeds to address the question through the wager argument, construing the question of whether or not to believe in God as a problem about which side of a bet to take. If I bet on God's existence, that is, if I believe in God, and God actually exists, I win eternal happiness; should I believe in God and he doesn't exist, then I don't win eternal happiness, but then I don't lose anything either. However, if I bet against God, that is, if I fail to believe in God, I risk losing the prize of infinite value that I could have won. Should God not exist, then I won't be any worse off than I would be if I believed in him and he didn't exist. But if I failed to believe in God and he *does* exist, then I will lose eternal happiness and be damned. If I am rational, then, I should believe in God.[4]

---

4   This, of course, is a very simplified version of Pascal's much more subtle argument. There is an enormous literature on Pascal's wager. A good account of the argument can be found in Ian Hacking, *The Emergence of Probability* (Cambridge: Cambridge University Press, 1975 and 2006), chap. 8. There are attacks on the cogency of the argument too numerous to cite here. But for the

The wager thus concludes that I should believe in God. But the 'should' here is a prudential 'should': in just the sense that I should chose a bet where I can expect the greater gain, I should chose to believe in God. But what exactly does this mean? How can I *choose* to believe in God? What if I can't? As I pointed out earlier, Pascal proposes a regimen, a way of life that I can consciously choose to adopt that, he claims, will result in my coming to have the faith that I seek:

> You would like to find faith and do not know the way? You would like to be cured of unbelief and ask for the remedies? Learn from those who were bound like you, and who now wager all they have. These are people who know the way you wish to follow, and who are cured of the illness of which you wish to be cured. Follow the way by which they began: they acted as if they believed, took holy water, had masses said, etc. This will make you believe naturally and mechanically [*vous abêtira*]. [S680/L418]

(This is what I will call the Pascal Regimen from now on.) What Pascal says in this quotation is interesting in and of itself. But more interesting still, Pascal claims, on at least some occasions, that when I enter into this regimen and follow it out, I

---

purposes of this essay, the problems with the argument are not at issue. My interest here is not with the wager argument itself, but what happens afterwards, when we have decided that we want to believe that God exists.

will have not only belief, but *rational* belief.[5] That is, I will come to see reasons that support my faith, reasons which are hidden to me before I enter into the regimen:

> "I do not ask you for blind faith." …
> "I do not intend you to submit your belief to me without reason, and I do not claim to subdue you by tyranny." I also do not claim to give you a reason for everything. To reconcile these oppositions, I intend to make you see clearly by convincing proofs, by marks of the divine in me that will convince you of what I am; and to establish my authority by marvels and proofs you cannot reject. You will then believe the things I teach, finding no ground for rejecting them, other than that you cannot by yourself tell whether they are true or not. [S182/L149]

Here things get a bit unclear to me. Divine grace seems to enter at this point, but how it enters is a bit perplexing. Sometimes Pascal speaks as if God

---

5 What I am putting forward is one strand in the text. We have to remember that the *Pensées* represents work in progress, notes for a book that was never written. While we can make out the general direction in which Pascal was heading, we shouldn't insist on consistency; there may be multiple paths that were still live possibilities at the time Pascal died. In any case, it doesn't matter for my purposes whether I am getting Pascal completely right from an historical point of view. My interests in this paper are to deal with an interesting philosophical problem that comes out of thinking about Pascal and his project in the *Pensées*.

gives his grace to all who genuinely seek him, and
the evidence is open to anyone who genuinely wants
to find God. The last passage I quoted continues
as follows:

> … Thus wanting to appear openly to those who seek
> him with all their heart and hidden from those who
> flee him with all their heart, God has tempered the
> knowledge of himself by giving signs of himself that
> are visible to those who seek him, and not by those
> who do not seek him.
>
> There is enough light for those who desire only
> to see and enough darkness for those of a contrary
> disposition. [S182/L149]

Elsewhere, though, grace seems to be less predict-
able and less dependent on what I do:

> The prophecies, the very miracles and proofs of
> our religion, are not of such a nature that it can
> be said that they are absolutely convincing; but
> they are also of such a kind that it cannot be said
> that it is unreasonable to believe them. Thus there
> is both evidence and obscurity, to enlighten some
> and to confuse others. But the evidence is such that
> it exceeds, or at least equals, the evidence to the
> contrary, so that reason cannot persuade us not to
> follow it, and thus it can only be concupiscence and
> malice of heart. And in this way there is enough
> evidence to condemn, and not enough to convince;
> and it seems that *those who follow it are motivated by
> grace and not reason*, and that those who shun it are
> motivated by concupiscence and not reason. [S423/
> L835; emphasis added]

This is what Pascal seems to have had in mind in a passage I quoted earlier:

> "Why, do you not yourself say that the sky and the birds prove God?" No. "And does not your religion say so?" No. For while this is true in a sense for some souls to whom God gave this illumination, nevertheless it is false for most of them. [S38/L3]

Now, this is an interesting and very powerful idea. Pascal's God doesn't ask for a blind faith: it is a faith supported by reasons. But these reasons can only be appreciated *after I am in a particular state of mind: only after I am committed to him, in a way, after I have already dedicated myself to the search for God, only after God has moved my heart.* Before I have faith, reason and experience are impotent, they are unable to give me real knowledge. But *after* the spiritual transformation, I am in a position to recognize the validity of the arguments for God's existence, the miracles and prophesies, the experience of nature itself. Only after the conversion can the believer appreciate the *rational* grounds of his or her faith.

In the end, then, after having gone through the process of conversion, I now seem to have rational belief, a belief in God that is supported by reasons that I consider rationally convincing. Even though the first steps toward this cognitive state—taking holy water and having masses said, in general behaving as if I were a believer—may not have been very promising, in the end, I seem to have reached a state in which I am *rationally entitled to believe that there is a God, as rationally entitled as I am about many others of the things I believe.* Or so it would seem.

But it is obvious that there is something funny about the way that I arrived at these supposedly rational beliefs, something unsettling about the process by which I fixed my belief. Should I rejoice that I have found God, and that I now see the truth, whereas before I was overcome by error? Or should I question my current epistemological state because of the way in which I attained it, because of its suspicious history?

Let's leave Pascal for the moment, and reflect on the kinds of problems that this case raises. First of all, I would like to sort through the jumble of different considerations that seem to be at play in this case. To sort out the issues, I want to put on the table some similar cases in which similar issues come up in somewhat different configurations. What we shall find, I think, is that there is no single issue that is causing us anxiety here. After this exploration I want to return to the Pascal case and face the hard question: how should we evaluate the apparently rational belief in God that I seem to have at the end of the Pascal regimen?

SELF-DECEPTION AND DECIDING TO BELIEVE

One obvious worry with the Pascal case is self-deception. I go into the Pascal Regimen with a strong desire to have a *specific* belief, to believe in the existence of God. I come out the other end with an actual belief in God. It is true that I also believe that I have good reasons for believing in the existence of God. But even so, one might worry that the desire had twisted my rational faculties, and that both the belief and the supposed reasons were just consequences of that strong desire. That is to say, I have managed to deceive myself.

Self-deception is not at all uncommon. Suppose that I have a number of friends who consider themselves wine connoisseurs. When I am at dinner with them, they go on and on about the wines that they drink, making subtle distinctions and claiming to discern all kinds of subtle aromas and tastes. I can tell the difference between a red and a white, between a Bordeaux and a Beaujolais on a good day, but I am very skeptical about all of this business, which strikes me as pretentious nonsense. However, my friends persuade me to go to wine tastings with them. I like their company and want to be accepted as part of the group, so skeptical as I am, I go with them once or twice a month. I go through the rituals, swishing the wine, putting it up to my nose, tasting it and listening to their incantations over the holy liquid. At first it is all nonsense to me. But after a while, I find that my perceptions change. I find that after a while, I, too, can participate in these discussions, and really taste what they claim is there. In fact, I get so good at it that I sometimes can convince my friends that they are wrong and I am right! The case is a bit different from the Pascal Regimen case: here there is no specific belief that I am trying to acquire. And it might really be the case that going to the wine class had helped me to sharpen my perception, and perceive things that are really in the wine, and make discriminations to which I was blind before. But we also need to take into account the real possibility of self-deception. The strong desire to impress my friends with my abilities as a wine connoisseur may well have twisted my judgment.

I don't doubt that self-deception might play a role in the Pascal case, as it might in the wine tasting case, but there are other reasons for being suspicious of the conversion that takes place as a result of the Pascal Regimen. Let me present some other cases similar to the Pascal Regimen where self-deception doesn't seem to play a role at all.

Suppose some neuropsychologists studied people undergoing the Pascal Regimen, and noticed that those whose beliefs were changed underwent distinctive chemical changes in their brain over the course of undergoing the regimen. Suppose, then, that they were able to design a pill that would produce, overnight, the same chemical changes: take one of these pills at night, and the next morning I am a Jansenist Catholic, just like Pascal, whatever my beliefs had been the night before, and whether or not I had any particular desire to become Catholic.

It seems plausible to me that if I took such a pill and woke up the next morning a believing Catholic, I should be somewhat suspicious of my beliefs, even if I also had some convincing arguments for believing that God exists. And my suspicions would have nothing to do with self deception: on my assumptions, the pill would work in exactly the same way, whatever my previous beliefs or desires were. That is to say, the fact that I *wanted* to be a believing Catholic would have no role to play in my new beliefs. There are worries, but they don't seem to be related to self-deception.

Here is another case, even closer to the Pascal Regimen. The case comes from a study by Tanya Luhrmann, as reported in her book, *Persuasions of the Witch's Craft: Ritual Magic in Contemporary England*. (Cambridge, MA: Harvard University Press, 1989). Luhrmann was a Ph.D. student in anthropology at Cambridge University in the early 1980s, fascinated by the fact that many apparently intelligent, university-trained people, many of whom were professionals, were active participants in the world of the occult and the magical. In order to study the phenomenon, she decided to enter into the occult world in 1980s England. Or better, she decided to enter into a number of those worlds; there isn't just one. And so, she did the equivalent of taking holy water and having masses said. She went to meetings, joined active groups, participated in their rituals. She read the magazines that they read, took the correspondence courses that they took to become qualified to advance in the hierarchy and become learned in things magical. In short, she lived the life that they did, entered into their practices.

But what for me is quite striking is the account that she gives of the cognitive state of the participants in this curious life. People who undergo the regimen, as she herself did, find themselves living in a different world. These experiences tended to confirm, for example, the efficacy of the magical ceremonies that the practitioners performed. Here is an instance she reports:

> Emily had been reading about magic for five years … when she decided to enter magic practice in earnest. She took a home study course … and became involved in discussion groups. She joined the Glittering Sword shortly before I did, and then joined a 'women's mysteries' group … . During the year in the *ad hoc* group, she performed rituals which she 'knew' were powerful. She said about one which she wrote that, 'I couldn't remember reading more than a third of it. Something else took over.' That ritual was about water: later, she remarked: 'and the results have been amazing. For a week everyone around me was bursting into tears or anger, and then it rained. There was water everywhere. When she went to study groups on divination, she was delighted with the high rate of her predictive success.… By the end of that year, Emily was quite sure that magic had

practical effects, and that magical forces were part of physical reality.[6]

In this way, the process of studying, attending ceremonies, slowly becoming a member of the community of magicians involves a real epistemic shift, literally a new way of seeing the world and a new conception of what is rational and reasonable. Luhrmann found that immersing oneself in the culture of magic—taking holy water and saying Black Masses—can cause a radical transformation in one's way of looking at the world, in just the way that the Pascal Regimen does.

Now, in the case of Luhrmann's subject Emily, one can well suppose that there was an element of self-deception involved. What draws people to want to make the effort of study and participation in the demanding rituals is the evident attractiveness of the world of the occult: there are obvious pleasures to be had in thinking that you live in a world of gods and goddesses, sorcerers and spirits, where magical rituals can connect you to the hidden powers that

---

6 *Persuasions*, pp. 285-86. It should be noted here that Luhrmann advances Emily as an example of someone who believes in the physical reality of magic, as real as the rest of the physical world. Not all do. As Luhrmann explains, some see it as an alternative parallel reality, or as symbolic.

rule the universe.[7] It is not implausible to assume that for many practitioners, their devotion to the regimen and their ultimate success at attaining the cognitive transformation is driven at least in part by their deep desire for it to be true.

So far we are in a situation very much like the Pascal Regimen, and one can wonder here about the element of self-deception. But here is where it gets interesting. Luhrmann followed out the same rituals not because she wanted to believe as her subjects did, but as a scientist studying their cognitive states and transformations. But yet she found her own epistemic state becoming transformed in exactly the same way as that of her subjects! She reports:

> … I … took the courses and attended the exercise groups one was meant to attend as a student of magic, and I discovered to my astonishment that if you visualized and meditated in the ways that you were taught, you had the darnedest experiences. Not often, perhaps, but occasionally, and those occasions were compelling. Some months into my training I woke up one morning and saw six druids standing by the window and beckoning to me. Sometimes I felt magical power move through me like an electric current. I had moments in which

---

7   See *Persuasions*, chap. 23 for Luhrmann's own rather more nuanced account of what draws people to these practices.

the living room faded and the ancient gods became
real, really real.[8]

Whatever moved Luhrmann to her new beliefs, it
wasn't a matter of self-deception. But yet, if we are
suspicious of Emily and of the person who under-
goes the Pascal Regimen, we should be suspicious
of her final belief state as well. Which is to say, as
with the "Catholic Pill," if there is a problem, it
isn't entirely due to the problem of self-deception.
Self-deception may be a factor, but there is more
at work here.

NON-COGNITIVITY AND CONTINGENCY

So, what other factors are at issue here? What else
is causing the worry? Well, one obvious issue is
the fact that the Pascal Regimen seems to be *non-
cognitive* in a clear way. That is to say, the change in
belief is caused not by some process of education,
study, training of the senses, etc., but because I
entered into certain practices such as going to mass
and taking holy water. Here the Pascal Regimen is
rather different from the case of my education in
wine: going to a class in wine appreciation involves

---

8   T.M. Luhrmann, "The Art of Hearing God: Absorp-
tion, Dissociation, and Contemporary American Spiri-
tuality," *Spiritus* 5 (2005), 133-157, quotation at p. 140.
This is a summary of some of the material contained in
the earlier book; cf. *Persuasions*, p. 319.

educating my senses and learning to notice things that I might have missed before. There is a real possibility of self-deception under certain circumstances, of course. But there is also the possibility that I am learning to recognize things that are really there through a kind of training and education which is not present in the case of the Pascal Regimen, or the "Catholic Pill." The witchcraft case is a bit more complicated insofar as the regimen there does involve a kind of study, reading the literature that modern witches read, taking correspondence courses and the like. But one might genuinely suspect that it is the participation in non-cognitive rituals that is doing the real work there.[9]

I have no doubt that the fact that the Pascal Regimen is non-cognitive has a role to play in understanding why I am suspicious about the beliefs

---

9   The distinction between a cognitive and a non-cognitive regimen is actually rather more subtle than this. As Tom Kelly suggested to me, the Pascal Regimen might work by eliminating the passions and prejudices that prevent me from seeing the validity of the arguments. This may have been the way Pascal himself thought of it; in one passage quoted above he does note that "concupiscence and malice of heart" [S423/L835] are responsible for my blindness to the existence of God. If the Pascal Regimen works in this way, it isn't at all clear whether to think of it as cognitive or non-cognitive. But I will assume that it doesn't work in this way, just to keep things simple. And however the Pascal Regimen works, the pill example certainly is non-cognitive.

and arguments that I have as a result. But I think that there is more to it than that. Implicit in the Pascal case is a certain kind of contingency. The Pascal Regimen makes me into a believing, perhaps rationally believing Catholic. But there are other regimens that I might have chosen as well. Study Talmud, go to synagogue, and keep kosher, and I will become a believing orthodox Jew. Go to a madrasah, pray in a mosque at all the required times of day, visit Mecca, and I will become a devout Moslem. Study magic and witchcraft, participate in the rites of my local coven, and I will become a believer in witchcraft and magic. Now, Pascal might argue, other regimens may lead me to *belief*, but only his regimen can lead me to *rational* belief. That is to say, follow Achmed Pascal's regimen and I become a Moslem, or Shlomo Pascal's regimen and I become a Jew. But when I am in those states, I don't have the *rational* belief that I do when I follow Blaise Pascal's regimen. If true, this would seem to give Blaise's regimen an advantage that the others don't: rational belief should trump mere faith. But as Tanya Luhrmann's magic case suggests, there is every reason to believe that the alternative regimens will lead me to beliefs as rational as the Pascal Regimen will.

Now, in the case of these alternative regimens, we are dealing with procedures that are as noncognitive as the original Pascal Regimen was. One might think that this kind of contingency is a feature of non-cognitive regimens alone, but that when we move to cognitive ways of changing our beliefs, there is only one way that it can turn out. But that isn't true.

In his *Discourse on the Method*, Descartes begins by talking about his days in school. Even though his teachers thought that he was very smart, and even though he went to one of the best schools in Europe, still he was dissatisfied, and eventually decided to leave his studies as early as he could, to go out into the larger world. There he discovered that other peoples in other countries had beliefs quite different from his own:

> ... so long as I merely considered the customs of other men, I found hardly any reason for confidence, for I observed in them almost as much diversity as I had found previously among the opinions of philosophers. In fact the greatest benefit I derived from these observations was that they showed me many things which, although seeming very extravagant and ridiculous to us, are nevertheless commonly accepted and approved in other great nations; and so I learned not to believe too firmly anything of which I had been persuaded only by example and custom.[10]

---

10   René Descartes, *Discours de la méthode* §1, translated in Descartes, *The Philosophical Writings of Descartes*, ed. and trans. John Cottingham, Robert Stoothoff, Dugald Murdoch, and Anthony Kenny (Cambridge: Cambridge University Press, 1984-91), vol. 1, p. 115.

In this way he came to see how many of our beliefs were due to the accident of our birth. Had we been born in other countries at other times, or educated by different teachers in different countries, our view of the world would be completely different. Had I been born in China 2000 years ago, or in the wilds of Brazil's Amazon region only fifty years ago, my beliefs would be entirely different than they are now. This fact, what I have called the contingency of our beliefs, caused Descartes, and perhaps should cause us as well, to call some of our own beliefs into doubt. This, even though we arrive at our beliefs through a process of education by which we consider arguments and evidence, a completely cognitive regimen. The very fact that we could have arrived at alternative beliefs by following an alternative cognitive regimen should give us some pause.

G.A. Cohen gives a very nice example of this. He reports that when he was young, he was faced with the choice of studying philosophy at Harvard or studying at Oxford. He chose Oxford. At Oxford, he was taught a way of doing philosophy that employed the distinction between analytic and synthetic truths. He was taught that in a fully cognitive way: through argument. However, he notes, had he gone to Harvard, he would have been taught by W.V.O. Quine and his students that the analytic-synthetic distinction is unfounded. And he would have been taught that in a fully cognitive way:

through argument. And he would have believed that.[11]

Now, the contingency of belief is certainly disturbing. But the more I think about it the more difficult I find it to put my finger on what exactly the problem is. The problem isn't simply the fact that there is an element of chance in the way I came to the beliefs that I have. Suppose that there are two copies of the Handbook of True Facts on the library shelf, one that does, indeed, have true facts, and one that has some mistakes. (It was withdrawn by the publisher after printing, but somehow, my library didn't get the word.) Even though it is a matter of chance that I picked up the right one, the one that truly had true facts, and read that Taipei is in Taiwan that doesn't seem to undermine my claim to knowledge, even though the other copy mistakenly says that Taipei is in New Jersey. It is a lucky thing that I picked up the right volume, but why should it matter that I might have picked up the mistaken volume? Perhaps the worry is that whichever volume I had chosen, I would have believed whatever it said, *not* because I have some reason to think that it is trustworthy, but simply because it is the one that I happened to choose first. And had I chosen the wrong one, I would have been mistaken. Which is to say, there doesn't seem to be any direct connection

11   See chap. 1 of G.A. Cohen, *If You're an Egalitarian, How Come You're So Rich?* (Cambridge, MA: Harvard University Press, 2000), esp. pp. 16-19.

between the process by which I fix my belief about where Taipei is, and the truth of the matter, that it is in Taiwan. And that seems disturbing. Adam Elga has made another suggestion. According to him, the contingency of my belief raises the possibility that my beliefs are determined at least in part by factors that "we ourselves would count as biasing or distorting," such as the improper influence of local authorities, teachers, etc. This offers another possible way of understanding what is disturbing about the contingency of belief.[12] I do admit that I am simply not sure what is wrong with contingency. But there does seem to be something wrong.

RATIONALITY AND HISTORY

Let me review where things stand. I began with the problem I face after Pascal's wager: I want to believe that God exists. I then follow the Pascal Regimen in order to acquire the belief. That is, I go to masses, take holy water, and behave as if I am a believer. As

---

12   This is from the handout to Elga's presentation to the Princeton Workshop on Religion and Epistemology held on 4/26/08. Elga also suggests another possible way of understanding the problem that contingency raises. On that view, I would have to have been lucky to have taken the correct path to knowledge, as opposed to one of the other possible paths that lead to error, and I have no reason to believe that I was lucky. But Elga seems unsure whether this argument is persuasive.

a result, I come to believe in God. But even more than that, I come to appreciate arguments for the existence of God that I didn't appreciate before. In this way, I seem to have not only belief, but *rational* belief.

Or do I? Should I question my new-found belief? Should I worry that I have led myself into error? In investigating this question, I have suggested that there are a number of reasons to question this new-found belief and the reasons that seem to support it.

(1) *Self-deception*: My strong desire to believe in God may be influencing the belief that I come to have, even if it isn't doing it consciously. This is similar to the case where I want to believe that I can tell the difference between a good wine and a mediocre wine, or to that of Tanya Luhrmann's subject Emily who believes in the efficacy of her magic.

(2) *A Non-cognitive way of belief formation*: The Pascal Regimen is non-cognitive in the sense that it changes my belief not through argument or training, but through some irrelevant mechanism, by going to masses and taking holy water. In this way it is like the "Catholic Pill," the pill I take at night to change my beliefs in the morning, or like the anthropologist who attends the magical rituals as part of her research, and, much to her surprise, comes out believing that they actually work.

(3) *Contingency*: If I follow the Pascal Regimen I come out with one set of beliefs, as a Catholic, whereas if I had followed a different regimen, I

would have come out with different beliefs. This is G.A. Cohen's situation with respect to the analytic/synthetic distinction: had he attended graduate school at Harvard rather than Oxford, he would have come out a skeptic about the distinction rather than an adherent. But this is also very close to a very general problem that we all face: many of our beliefs, religious, scientific, and otherwise would be very different had we been born in a different place or at a different time, or had we been educated by different parents and different teachers. I admit that I don't know exactly what is problematic here, but there does seem to be something problematic.

It is important to note that these problems seem to be independent of one another: there seem to be instances of belief and belief formation that exhibit one problem but not the others, as I emphasized when I discussed them earlier. But what is interesting here is that the Pascal Regimen exhibits all of them: it seems open to the possibility of self-deception, it involves an entirely non-cognitive mode of belief formation, *and* it is contingent in the sense that had I adopted a different regimen, I would very likely have ended up at a rather different and incompatible epistemic state. Which is to say, there are multiple reasons for being cautious about accepting our final state of belief.

But what should I do in response to these problems? How should I treat my new-found belief in the existence of God, and the new arguments that now strike me as convincing? Is it rational for me to hang onto them? Or should I try to set them aside in some way?

Before addressing the problem, let me reformulate it a bit. Now, when we are thinking about the rationality of holding a belief, we must think about the rational considerations that weigh for and against it. Are there good arguments in either direction? What about empirical evidence? How much is there, and how strong is it? Having good arguments and good evidence for a belief would seem to make it rational, at least *prima facie* rational. But it is also important to know something about the history of our beliefs and the way in which we came to hold them and the way in which we came to think them rational. Our beliefs may be rational in the sense of being supported by evidence and argument, yet there may be radically different ways of getting to the very same epistemic state, at least some of which may possibly undermine or even defeat the *prima facie* rationality that comes from evidence and argument. Earlier we examined with some care the Pascal Regimen by which I get to that state with respect to a belief in the existence of God, and we have examined other ways of getting to beliefs which share important characteristics with the Pascal Regimen. But there are other ways of getting to a state in which we have beliefs supported by evidence and argument that would also seem to raise epistemological questions.[13] One way we can come to fix a belief involves looking assiduously for evidence for and against, carefully weighing the quality of the evidence, etc. Sometimes that's just what we do. On the other hand, sometimes we cut corners a bit, and look only for evidence in favor of a pet theory. Sometimes we may even go out of our way *not* to have to deal with contrary evidence by purposefully refraining to look places where we might find it. Sometimes belief (and the evidence that we take to support it) just comes to us from reading books, or going to class and listening to a teacher, or from what our parents taught us. Here we never go out and look for the evidence and argument that will make the belief rational; it is, as it were, handed to us on a silver platter. All these paths may eventuate in belief supported by evidence and argument, belief that is, in a sense, rational belief. In fact, all of these paths may lead to exactly the same belief, supported by exactly the same evidence. *But the history matters.* To the extent to which we think a history is appropriate or inappropriate for placing us in the state

---

13   In what follows I am drawing on some observations that Tom Kelly made in his essay, "Disagreement, Dogmatism, and Belief Polarization," forthcoming in *Journal of Philosophy*. In that paper, Kelly explores ways in which the prior commitment to a certain belief can bias the way in which we evaluate new evidence for and against that belief.

in question, that should have some effect on the rationality of the belief.

In this way, perhaps we can think of there being two aspects to the question of the rationality of belief in general, and this belief in particular: there is the rationality (or, at least, the *prima facie* rationality) that comes from having good evidence and good arguments, and there is the rationality that comes from the way in which we arrived at the evidence and arguments. Both are important.[14] One produces what we might call first-order rationality, the other what we might call second-order rationality. First-order rationality can be thought of in traditional terms as evidence and arguments that relate to the belief in question and give it at least a *prima facie* rationality. Second-order rationality relates to second-order considerations about how it was that

14 This is very much like the standard distinction in Bayesian (probabilistic) epistemology between synchronic and diachronic rationality, that is, rationality at a given time vs. rational belief change. A belief function is generally taken to be synchronically rational if it satisfies the standard Kolmogorov axioms for probability theory. A change in a belief function is taken to be diachronically rational when it proceeds by way of an appropriate rule, for example through conditionalization on new evidence. On this see William Talbott, "Bayesian Epistemology," *The Stanford Encyclopedia of Philosophy (Fall 2008 Edition)*, Edward N. Zalta (ed.), URL = <http://plato.stanford.edu/archives/fall2008/entries/epistemology-bayesian/>.

we came to find ourselves in the position in which we have a first-order rational belief. And the two can diverge. A belief can be first-order rational, at least *prima facie* rational in the sense of being supported by arguments and evidence without being second-order rational.[15]

And with this we can come back to the question I raised earlier, but now reformulated: how do these two aspects of rationality interact? In the particular case at hand, how should the discovery that my belief in the existence of God, a belief grounded in evidence and arguments, be affected by the fact that it has a problematic history?

Under certain circumstances, the second-order considerations may well undermine the *prima facie* rationality that accrues to my belief because of the evidence and arguments that we have. It is generally agreed that when forming our beliefs, we have some obligation to take account of all the evidence that is readily available, and not just select evidence or arguments that favor a view that we want to hold. Certainly, if the history of my current epistemic state were such that I could be justly accused of will-fully ignoring unfavorable evidence and arguments that counted against my belief, then second-order considerations would undermine the *prima facie* rationality of my belief. But there are cases of less

---

15 I can't see how a belief can be second-order rational while being first-order irrational, but that may just be a limitation on my imagination.

blatant bias at the second order that would also undermine the first-order rationality. Suppose that I depended on what was generally considered to be an objective and unbiased journalistic source for my beliefs about global warming, and on the basis of that came to the view that global warming was a natural process that isn't a causal consequence of human activity. If I were to discover that the source was funded by oil and gas companies, and simply reported evidence consistent with their point of view while suppressing contrary evidence, then my belief, which had been first-order rational would be undermined. Or, I might come to realize that my own ways of forming belief were somehow biased in favor of one or another side of the debate. If the bias wasn't conscious and deliberate, I may not be blameworthy in holding the belief that global warming was a purely natural process. But, at the same time, as soon as I came to realize the bias in my epistemic practices, my belief would be undermined and would no longer be rational.[16] One can debate just how far considerations like this can go. Seeking new evidence isn't cost free. Just how much am I obligated to search out *all* possible evidence for and against? And how assiduous do I have to be in examining possible biases in my methods for fixing belief? If I read one book on climate change, do I have to read all the others? If I study Western

---

16   This is the kind of case that Tom Kelly considers in "Disagreement."

science, do I have to look at all of the alternative systems available? While answers to these questions are not clear, it is clear that one way or another, these considerations are relevant to the first-order rationality of belief.

These considerations don't seem to be at issue in the case of the Pascal Regimen; the kinds of second-order problems that we discussed earlier with respect to the Pascal Regimen don't directly imply that my evidence is biased or the arguments one-sided. What they suggest is a more general and perhaps more insidious, but somewhat vaguer infirmity in my reasons for belief, that somehow or another I have been misled into accepting arguments and evidences for belief that don't really give adequate support to my belief. Doubts raised by the kinds of second-order considerations we discussed earlier just *may* cause me to go back and look more carefully at the arguments and evidences I have for my beliefs. When I do so, I just *may* find that they aren't as strong as I had originally thought they were, and in that way, my doubts may lead me to withdraw my claim that my belief is rational. Tanya Luhrmann's Emily, for example, reflecting on how she came to magic might reconsider the evidence that she thought that she had for the efficacy of the rituals that she performed, and come to realize that it isn't as strong and convincing as she had originally thought. In that case her first-order epistemic state would have been changed as a result of contemplat-

ing her second-order epistemic situation, though
not directly. Similarly, reflecting on the fact that my
belief in God, together with the reasons that I have
for it is a result of the Pascal Regimen might well
lead me to go back and rethink the reasons I came
to have for that belief, and might eventually lead me
to see flaws in them that I didn't see before. In that
way, realizing that my belief in God is second-order
irrational might lead me to lose faith in my evidence
or call my arguments into doubt through a process
of reexamination and reflection, and in this way
may lead me to suspend judgment on the question
of the existence of God.

But it need not happen in this way. It doesn't
seem unreasonable to suppose that I might remain
convinced by my arguments and evidence, even after
reflecting on the suspicious elements of the history
that led me there, and even after subjecting them to
greater scrutiny. That is, when contemplating the
arguments for the existence of God that I came to
find convincing after undergoing the Pascal Regimen, they might well still seem sound and valid to
me, and retain their power to convince. Or when
looking about at nature, and contemplating the
beauty and order in the world, I might still see it
as powerful evidence that there is a God standing
behind it all. All of this with full awareness of the
problematic history of these epistemic attitudes.
What then?

Under these circumstances, I can't just dismiss
the second-order considerations that we discussed
earlier; they are still there and still worrisome. And
they should cause me to worry about the solidity of
my beliefs. But the nature of the doubt is different
than the situation in which the second-order doubts
lead me to question or even withdraw my reasons
for believing that God exists. On this different sce-
nario, I remain convinced when I contemplate the
evidence and the arguments, but, at the same time,
the second-order doubts should cause me to worry
whether I may be under the spell of a cognitive
illusion, a kind of reasoning that has all the apparent marks of truth and leads to a subjective feeling
of conviction and certainty, but hides a fallacy of
some sort that is not evident.[17] This worry, though,
serious as it may be and disturbing as it may be,
doesn't necessarily shake the feeling of confidence:
be it a genuine argument or a cognitive illusion,
I may well remain convinced even in the face of
second-order doubt. And I will still have *reasons*
for my conviction. Though I may worry that they
might be illusory, I don't *know* that they are, and
cannot just set those reasons aside. Nor is there any
straightforward way of establishing whether or not
they are illusory, as one can usually do in the case

---

17   On the notion of a cognitive illusion, see the essays
in Rüdiger Pohl, ed., *Cognitive Illusions: A Handbook on
Fallacies and Biases in Thinking, Judgment and Memory*
(Hove, London and New York: Psychology Press, 2004).

of an optical illusion.[18] In a certain sense, this is the situation we are in with many of our beliefs, which also share the infirmities we have found in the belief in the existence of God that derives from the Pascal Regimen. Some we hold in part because we *want* them to be true, whether or not we have sufficient grounds for holding them. Some we hold because of non-cognitive processes that are not unlike the ones involved in the Pascal Regimen; indeed, I strongly suspect that for many people, their religious beliefs are a direct result of something very much like the Pascal Regimen, though not entered into with the conscious determination to fix religious belief. And finally, and most importantly, a great many of our beliefs and even the arguments that we find convincing are shaped by contingent factors, factors that arise out of the accidents of our education and upbringing. Indeed, our whole conception of the world is shaped by the historical accident of having been born when we were, in the countries and cultures where we were, and educated by the parents and teachers we happened to have. But even

---

18   Consider the well-known Müller-Lyer illusion, lines of the same length with arrows at each end, where in one case the arrows point in, in the other they point out. To most observers, the line with the arrows pointing in looks longer than the line with the arrows pointing out. However, a quick check with a ruler can establish that the lines are really the same length. Cognitive illusions are generally more difficult to undermine.

when we reflect on the history of our beliefs, we still find the them and the reasons we have for believing them compelling, and most of us are strongly disinclined to toss them aside and start over again, as Descartes, for example, would have us do.

Let me elaborate a bit on this. When we reflect on the state of science in Pascal's day, it is interesting to observe that figures such as Galileo, Huygens, Boyle and Descartes were quite confident that they had figured out the main features of the physical world, as confident as we are today that we have. But they were wrong. To be sure, each had insights that proved to be durable, and discovered things about the world that we still think are true. But each also held things that we now think are mistaken. Furthermore, even though there may be continuity between their science and ours, no one at the time could predict which aspects of their world-views would survive, and which wouldn't. And when we reflect on the fact that in three or four hundred years, the scientists of the future will see our own errors in just the way we see the errors of past scientists, that should make us somewhat uncomfortable. Because of the accidents of birth and upbringing, we may well be ensnared in cognitive illusions that we just cannot see, and cannot escape. This has been called the "pessimistic induction" by philosophers of science.[19] Yet it seems unreasonable for us to reject modern science just because of that: when we contemplate the reasons we have for holding our current view of the world, we remain convinced, and, it seems to me, we are rational to do so. But yet we cannot simply set aside the possibility that we are deeply mistaken in some way that is now impossible for us to see. This, in a way, is exactly the position I am suggesting that I might find myself after undergoing the Pascal Regimen, convinced by my reasons for believing that God exists while at the same time having reasons to believe that I might well be caught in a cognitive illusion, without any way of resolving the question.

What, then, am I to do? Let me focus back on the belief in the existence of God, and on the Pascal Regimen by which I came to it. In the circumstances that I am considering here, there is a sense in which I cannot doubt my belief in God, at least while con-

---

19   There is a large literature on the pessimistic induction and its supposed implications, particularly for the question of scientific realism. On this, see, e.g., Peter Godfrey-Smith, *Theory and Reality* (Chicago: University of Chicago Press, 1993), pp. 177f. The *locus classicus* for the argument is Larry Laudan, "A Confutation of Convergent Realism," *Philosophy of Science* 48 (1981), pp. 19-49. I am not interested in scientific realism, but simply in a circumstance where we can maintain our rational conviction in a belief in the face of legitimate worries about whether we might be caught in a cognitive illusion.

templating the evidence and arguments: despite the
second-order doubts, the reasons for belief remain
convincing. But, at the same time, there is a sense in
which I am *obligated* to doubt my belief: in the face
of my awareness of the problematic history of my
belief, along with the reasons for my belief, I cannot
blithely put my full trust in my belief in God either.

Here is a way of thinking about what I should do
in this circumstance. It might be appropriate here
to recall what David Hume wrote about what he
called mitigated skepticism in his *Enquiry concerning
Human Understanding*:

> The greater part of mankind are naturally apt to
> be affirmative and dogmatical in their opinions;
> and while they see objects only on one side, and
> have no idea of any counterpoising argument, they
> throw themselves precipitately into the principles,
> to which they are inclined; nor have they any indul-
> gence for those who entertain opposite sentiments.
> … But could such dogmatical reasoners become
> sensible of the strange infirmities of human under-
> standing, even in its most perfect state, and when
> most accurate and cautious in its determinations;
> such a reflection would naturally inspire them with
> more modesty and reserve, and diminish their fond
> opinion of themselves, and their prejudice against
> antagonists. … In general, there is a degree of doubt,
> and caution, and modesty, which, in all kinds of

scrutiny and decision, ought for ever to accompany a just reasoner.[20]

What Hume proposes here is a kind of epistemic modesty: in reaction to the deep infirmities that might lie hidden in our beliefs and in the way in which we come to them, he suggests not that we reject our beliefs, but that we adopt a degree of doubt and caution. This, I think, is the attitude that I have to adopt in the case at hand, where despite the second-order infirmities, I still find my reasons for belief compelling. This epistemic modesty might be manifested in a number of ways. Even though I may continue to find the first-order reasons for my belief compelling, if I have second-order doubts I might not put as much trust in it in practical situations. That is to say, I might act as if it could be false in situations where its truth or falsity had important consequences on the outcome of our actions. In addition I might be more willing to give it up under certain situations. That is, I might be more open to contrary evidence or arguments than I might otherwise be.[21] Or I might subject the evidence

---

20   David Hume, *Enquiry Concerning Human Understanding* § 12.3.

21   Brian Skyrms has tried to capture this idea in a probabilistic context with his conception of resiliency. See "Resiliency, Propensity, and Causal Necessity," *Journal of Philosophy* 74 (1977), pp. 704-13. A belief is more or less resilient to the extent that new contrary disconfirming evidence will decrease its degree of belief. For an

and arguments that support it to (still) more criti-
cal scrutiny. That is, I might take it upon myself to
look yet more carefully for additional reasons for or
against, to look for paralogisms in my arguments or
weaknesses in my evidences than I might if I weren't
worried about its epistemic status. But one thing
that Hume does *not* recommend is that I give up
my belief: though held with a spirit of epistemic
modesty, it is held nevertheless.

In the specific case at hand the moral is that I
need not give up the epistemic state that I arrive at
the end of the regimen that Pascal proposes: after
going to mass, taking holy water, acting like the
faithful, I have attained a state of belief in God for
which I think that I have good reason. I have not
only faith, but the arguments to support that faith.
In that state I should delight in my luck at having
found what I am convinced is the truth. And to the
extent that I have not found specific reasons to reject
either the evidence or the arguments, I can say that
my belief in the existence of God is rational. This
is what I have called first-order rationality. But, at
the same time, the general flaws I have found in
this final epistemic state should cause me to admit

---

interesting application of this idea to a practical case not
unlike the ones examined here, where we have reason to
distrust the reliability of one of our belief-forming faculties, in particular memory, see Andy Egan and Adam
Elga, "I Can't Believe I'm Stupid," *Philosophical Perspectives* 19 (2005), pp. 77-93.

my fallibility, and induce me to walk with care, constantly reviewing and rethinking my views and the arguments that seem to support them, cause me to hesitate before putting my full trust in them in practical circumstances. This reflects the second-order irrationality of my epistemic state.

But is this attitude coherent? Epistemological modesty of the sort that Hume recommends is certainly commendable; it would seem to be a good thing to continue to review our evidence and arguments, to search for flaws in them and for better ones. And it would seem to be reasonable to be cautious about whether or not we should actually act on beliefs about which we had the kinds of doubts that I called second-order. But isn't this just to say that I am calling the state of belief arrived at through the Pascal Regimen into doubt? Indeed, why aren't I rationally obligated to suspend judgment about the existence of God under these circumstances? In what sense can I separate the rational conviction I supposedly have that God exists, a rational conviction that I arrived at through the Pascal Regimen, from the doubt that arises from the reflections on its history?

To address this question, let me turn to Frank Ramsey. In his celebrated essay, "Truth and Probability," Ramsey is interested in the question as to how to measure degrees of belief. In the course of his discussion, he writes:

We can, in the first place, suppose that the degree of a belief is something perceptible by its owner; for instance that beliefs differ in the intensity of a feeling by which they are accompanied, which might be called a belief-feeling or feeling of conviction, and that by the degree of belief we mean the intensity of this feeling. This view would be very inconvenient, for it is not easy to ascribe numbers to the intensities for feelings. ... We are driven therefore to the second supposition that the degree of a belief is a causal property of it, which we can express vaguely as the extent to which we are prepared to act on it. This is a generalization of the well-known view, that the differentia of belief lies in its causal efficacy....[22]

Ramsey's project in this essay is to set out a notion of degree of belief in a given proposition p that is understood in terms of our willingness to act on p, where that is understood in terms of the odds on bets an agent would be willing to take, where the outcome of the bet is determined by the truth or falsity of p; in this way Ramsey explicitly endorses "the old-established way of measuring a belief [which] is to propose a bet, and see what are the lowest odds which he will accept."[23] Ramsey wants to substitute this conception of degree of belief

---

22 "Truth and Probability," in F.P. Ramsey, ed. D.H. Mellor, *Foundations: Essays in Philosophy, Logic, Mathematics and Economics* (Atlantic Highlands, NJ: Humanities Press, 1978), pp. 58-100, quotation from p. 71.

23 "Truth and Probability," p. 74.

for a conception which proposes that we think of degree of belief in terms of the introspectively felt intensity of the belief.

I certainly agree that the notion of belief that Ramsey adopts, which links degree of belief, indeed, belief itself to a disposition to behave in a particular way is an interesting and rich notion of belief. But that doesn't mean that we should give up the idea that there is a feeling of conviction associated with certain propositions, a feeling that is accessible to us through introspection. Ramsey is certainly right to be skeptical that we can quantify this conception of belief, that we could apply some numerical scale to this intensity in a meaningful way. And no doubt there are other problems that we would have to confront. But *prima facie*, it seems to me that the felt intensity of conviction is a real phenomenon in our epistemological lives, and that it has a role to play in yes/no belief and reasoning, even if it isn't of much use in more quantitative approaches to belief such as the Bayesian epistemology to which Ramsey contributed so much. Ramsey considered it as a competitor to the conception of belief that he was setting out in his essay. But it seems to me that it can better be regarded as a complementary conception of belief, a different conception that captures other aspects of our mental and episte-mological lives. And if these two conceptions of belief are really distinct from one another, as I think that they are, then they can diverge. In particular, it

may be possible for us to have a feeling of conviction, indeed, a feeling of conviction that is rational
in the sense that it is grounded in reasons, while,
at the same time, having a Ramsey-style degree of
belief in it that is less than one.[24] To bring this back
to the question at hand, I can have conviction that
God exists, *real* conviction that God exists, while
at the same time being somewhat reluctant to act
on it insofar as I realize that that conviction may
possibly be grounded in a cognitive illusion.

(I might observe here that the situation is somewhat like the situation that Descartes' meditator
is in after the first Meditation, and before proving
that God exists. He has come to believe that his
cognitive faculties may lead him astray because he
was created by a deceiving God or by chance. This
does not prevent him from having beliefs, such as
the 'cogito' that are fully convincing to him; indeed,
it is through such beliefs that he will be led to true
knowledge. But it at the same time he cannot say

---

24 In a similar way, Michael Bratman draws a distinction between what we believe, and what we take for
granted in different circumstances. We may believe that
the ladder is sound, but in a practical situation when we
need to use it, we may not take it for granted. See his
essay, "Practical Reasoning and Acceptance in a Context,"
Mind 101 (1992), pp. 1-15, esp. p. 7; reprinted as chap.
2 of his *Faces of Intention: Selected Essays on Intention
and Agency* (Cambridge: Cambridge University Press,
1999), p. 24.

for sure that they are true until he proves that God exists and is not a deceiver.[25])

So, when we reflect on the history of our beliefs, does that cause us to doubt our beliefs, to hold them with a lower degree of certainty? Yes, and no. 'Yes' in the sense that we may be less willing, even much less willing to act on our beliefs. That is to say that reflecting on the history of our beliefs may lead us to attribute to them Ramsey degrees of belief significantly below one. In addition it might also lead us to rethink our evidence and arguments for them, to look for more evidence or better arguments and the like, and in that way may eventually lead

---

25   On this, see Harry Frankfurt, *Demons, Dreamers and Madmen: The Defense of Reason in Descartes'* Meditations (Princeton: Princeton University Press, 2008), chap. 14, esp. pp. 226f. Frankfurt points out that for Descartes, clear and distinct perceptions are absolutely irresistible while we are having them, but it is only when we are at some distance from a clear and distinct perception that we can call it into doubt and raise the question as to whether or not everything we clearly and distinctly perceive is actually true. This, he claims, is why Descartes appeals to memory in the course of his validation of reason: it allows us to consider clear and distinct perceptions at a moment when we are not actually perceiving them clearly and distinctly. and thus incapable of doubting them. In this way he rejects readings of Descartes' validation of reason project on which what Descartes is doing is validating memory: memory as such has only an instrumental role in Descartes' argument.

us to alter our first-order epistemic state. But 'no' in the sense that it may not decrease the feeling of conviction with which we hold them. When I contemplate my reasons for believing in God, to take the example under consideration, I cannot help but remain confident in that belief, and even feel that that conviction is rational.

LAST THOUGHTS

At the very beginning of this essay I raised the following question: can I trust the belief that comes out of the regimen that I enter into as a result of Pascal's Wager? When I reach the end state of Pascal Regimen, and have faith in God grounded in reasons, am I really entitled to belief? At this point, we can answer that yes, in a sense I am: I have a feeling of conviction based on evidence, and that is a kind of certainty to which I am entitled, in a sense. But, at the same time, I shouldn't act on it and I shouldn't rest with it. Because of the reasonable fear that I am in the grips of a cognitive illusion, I should continue to examine my reasons for belief, and continue to hunt for good reasons both to believe in God and not to believe in God. And while I am doing this, I should hesitate to give full trust to it in practical situations, and hedge my bets. My belief may indeed be grounded on a cognitive illusion, and I should be cautious. I should continue to believe, but, at the same time, I should exhibit epistemological modesty, as Hume recommends. Indeed, this is true not only for the conclusion that God exists, which I have arrived at by way of the Pascal Regimen, but more generally for many of my beliefs, beliefs many of which I hold simply because I want them to be true, or because I grew up where I did and was taught by the teachers and parents who taught me, beliefs I hold because of the particular social conditioning that I happen to have undergone.

In this way, I am left in an interesting position. Through the wager argument I am led to undertake a regimen that will lead me to belief in God, indeed, a kind of rational belief in God. However, I have argued, even though I have a kind of certainty, at the same time I should be cautious about acting on it without reservation: despite the internal feeling of conviction, I have to worry about whether I may be caught in the trap of a cognitive illusion. In practical situations, in daily life, then, I should act with care. Now, it is notoriously difficult to see into the mind of God and say for sure how he will react to this situation. But, it seems to me that the conviction I have may well suffice for the salvation that I seek, the salvation that was the ultimate point of this whole exercise. And this leads to a delicious irony. It is possible that while the certainty that I arrive at through the Pascal Regimen may be good enough for eternal salvation, it isn't good enough for everyday life.[26]

---

26 This essay picks up roughly where I left off in "*Religio philosophi*: Some Thoughts on God, Reason, and Faith," in Louise Antony, ed., *Philosophers Without God: Meditations on Atheism and the Secular Life* (Oxford: Oxford University Press, 2007), pp. 32-40. Earlier (and much cruder) versions of this lecture were given at the University of South Florida, as the Charles McCracken Lecture at Michigan State University, at the University of Washington, the National Cheng-chih University (Taipei, Taiwan), the National Chung-cheng University (Chiayi, Taiwan), and the Princeton/Bucharest Seminar in Early Modern Thought (Malancrav Manor, Transylvania, Romania). I would like to thank the audiences at those presentations for what were always lively discussions. As the essay evolved from an historical essay to an essay in epistemology, I felt a strong need to get the advice of some colleagues in contemporary theory of knowledge. I would like to thank Adam Elga, Tom Kelly, Frank Jackson, and Ernie Sosa for discussing the issues with me, and for their comments on earlier drafts of this essay. They may not agree with where I wound up in the end, but the essay is vastly better because of their interventions.

The Aquinas Lectures
Published by the Marquette University Press
Milwaukee WI 53201-3141

1. *St. Thomas and the Life of Learning.* John F. McCormick, S.J. (1937) ISBN 0-87462-101-1

2. *St. Thomas and the Gentiles.* Mortimer J. Adler (1938) ISBN 0-87462-102-X

3. *St. Thomas and the Greeks.* Anton C. Pegis (1939) ISBN 0-87462-103-8

4. *The Nature and Functions of Authority.* Yves Simon (1940) ISBN 0-87462-104-6

5. *St. Thomas and Analogy.* Gerald B. Phelan (1941) ISBN 0-87462-105-4

6. *St. Thomas and the Problem of Evil.* Jacques Maritain (1942) ISBN 0-87462-106-2

7. *Humanism and Theology.* Werner Jaeger (1943) ISBN 0-87462-107-0

8. *The Nature and Origins of Scientism.* John Wellmuth (1944) ISBN 0-87462-108-9

9. *Cicero in the Courtroom of St. Thomas Aquinas.* E.K. Rand (1945) ISBN 0-87462-109-7

10. *St. Thomas and Epistemology.* Louis-Marie Regis, O.P. (1946) ISBN 0-87462-110-0

11. *St. Thomas and the Greek Moralists.* Vernon J. Bourke (1947) ISBN 0-87462-111-9

12. *History of Philosophy and Philosophical Education.* Étienne Gilson (1947) ISBN 0-87462-112-7

13. *The Natural Desire for God.* William R. O'Connor (1948) ISBN 0-87462-113-5

14. *St. Thomas and the World State.* Robert M. Hutchins (1949) ISBN 0-87462-114-3

15. *Method in Metaphysics.* Robert J. Henle, S.J. (1950) ISBN 0-87462-115-1

16. *Wisdom and Love in St. Thomas Aquinas.* Étienne Gilson (1951) ISBN 0-87462-116-X

17. *The Good in Existential Metaphysics.* Elizabeth G. Salmon (1952) ISBN 0-87462-117-8

18. *St. Thomas and the Object of Geometry.* Vincent E. Smith (1953) ISBN 0-87462-118-6

19. *Realism And Nominalism Revisted.* Henry Veatch (1954) ISBN 0-87462-119-4

20. *Imprudence in St. Thomas Aquinas.* Charles J. O'Neil (1955) ISBN 0-87462-120-8

21. *The Truth That Frees.* Gerard Smith, S.J. (1956) ISBN 0-87462-121-6

22. *St. Thomas and the Future of Metaphysics.* Joseph Owens, C.Ss.R. (1957) ISBN 0-87462-122-4

23. *Thomas and the Physics of 1958: A Confrontation.* Henry Margenau (1958) ISBN 0-87462-123-2

24. *Metaphysics and Ideology.* Wm. Oliver Martin (1959) ISBN 0-87462-124-0

25. *Language, Truth and Poetry.* Victor M. Hamm (1960) ISBN 0-87462-125-9

50. *Imagination and Metaphysics in St. Augustine.* Robert O'Connell, S.J. (1986) ISBN 0-87462-227-1

51. *Expectations of Immortality in Late Antiquity.* Hilary A Armstrong (1987) ISBN 0-87462-154-2

52. *The Self.* Anthony Kenny (1988) ISBN 0-87462-155-0

53. *The Nature of Philosophical Inquiry.* Quentin Lauer, S.J. (1989) ISBN 0-87562-156-9

54. *First Principles, Final Ends and Contemporary Philosophical Issues.* Alasdair MacIntyre (1990) ISBN 0-87462-157-7

55. *Descartes among the Scholastics.* Marjorie Greene (1991) ISBN 0-87462-158-5

56. *The Inference That Makes Science.* Ernan McMullin (1992) ISBN 0-87462-159-3

57. *Person and Being.* W. Norris Clarke, S.J. (1993) ISBN 0-87462-160-7

58. *Metaphysics and Culture.* Louis Dupré (1994) ISBN 0-87462-161-5

59. *Mediæval Reactions to the Encounters between Faith and Reason.* John F. Wippel (1995) ISBN 0-87462-162-3

60. *Paradoxes of Time in Saint Augustine.* Roland J. Teske, S.J. (1996) ISBN 0-87462-163-1

61. *Simplicity As Evidence of Truth.* Richard Swinburne (1997) ISBN 0-87462-164-X

62. *Science, Religion and Authority: Lessons from the Galileo Affair.* Richard J. Blackwell. (1998) ISBN 0-87462-165-8

63. *What Sort of Human Nature? Medieval Philosophy and the Systematics of Christology.* Marilyn McCord Adams. (1999) ISBN 0-87462-166-6

64. *On Inoculating Moral Philosophy against God.* John M. Rist. (2000) ISBN 0-87462-167-X.

65. *A Sensible Metaphysical Realism.* William P. Alston (2001) ISBN 0-87462-168-2.

66. *Eschatological Themes in Medieval Jewish Philosophy.* Arthur Hyman. (2002) ISBN 0-87462-169-0

67. *Old Wine in New Skins.* Jorge J. E. Gracia. (2003) ISBN 0-87462-170-4.

68. *The Metamorphoses of Phenomenological Reduction.* Jacques Tamininaux. (2004) ISBN 0-87462-171-2.

69. *Common Sense: A New Look at an Old Philosophical Tradition.* Nicholas Rescher. (2005) ISBN-13: 978-0-87462-172-3.

70. *Five Metaphysical Paradoxes.* Howard P. Kainz. (2006) ISBN 978-0-87462-173-0.

www.marquette.edu/mupress/

ISBN-13: 978-0-87462-176-1
ISBN-10: 0-87462-176-3